THE
FIRST STORYBOOK
OF NUMBERS

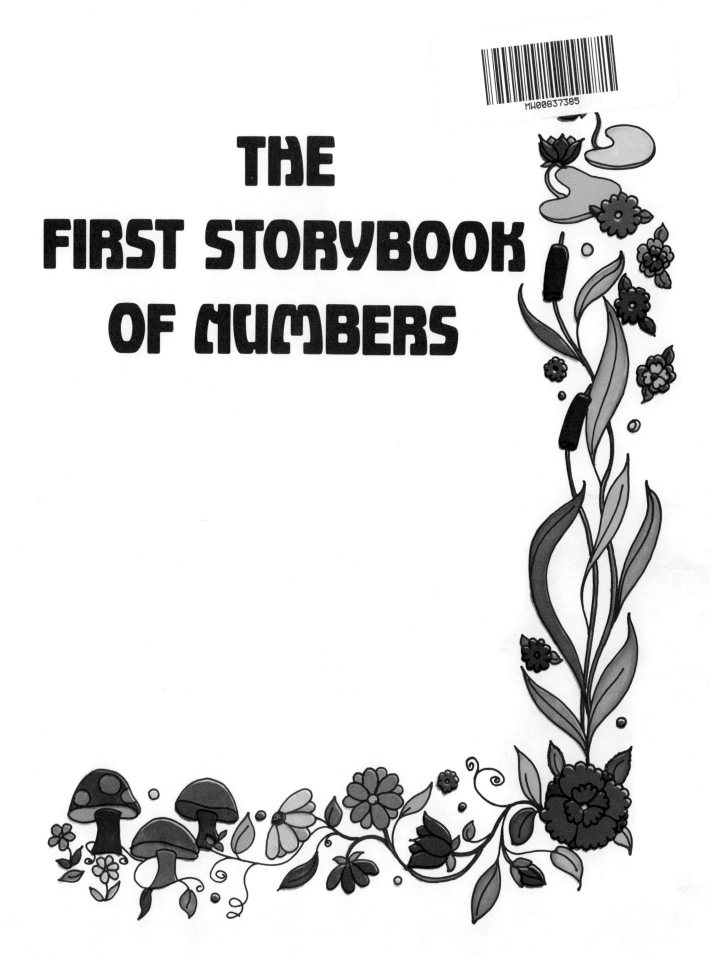

Copyright © MCMLXXIX by Banner Press, Inc.
All rights reserved.
This edition is published by Derrydale Books,
a division of Crown Publishers, Inc.,
by arrangement with Banner Press, Inc.
a   b   c   d   e   f   g   h
DERRYDALE 1979 EDITION
Manufactured in the United States of America

Library of Congress Cataloging in Publication Data
The First storybook of numbers.
    SUMMARY: Fairy tales, nursery rhymes, songs,
poems, riddles, and activities introduce the numbers
0 through 10, writing numerals, counting, and
comparing quantities.
    1. Numeration—Juvenile literature.
[1. Number concept. 2. Counting]
QA141.3.F57   513'.2   79-53950
ISBN 0-517-29546-6

INTRODUCTION

The First Storybook of Numbers introduces young children to the numbers zero through ten. It is designed to help children feel comfortable with numbers and understand the concepts behind them. There is a storybook, for reading, followed by a workbook, for practice. Ideally, they should be used in this order, the storybook preparing the way for the workbook. Once a child has progressed to the workbook, he or she should return to the storybook often, for both pleasure and the opportunity to try out new skills.

The storybook section begins with three of the best-loved fairy tales, told for the first time to emphasize numbers. By appearing in this context of fantasy and wonder, everyday numbers take on a new interest. Children will be mesmerized by giants and witches and angels at the same time they are becoming aware of the number of golden eggs and beautiful swans and gingerbread cookies.

Numbers also play an important part in the classic nursery rhymes, poems, and riddles that follow the fairy tales. Children learn and repeat these lyrical verses easily, and while they are learning the verses, they are also learning the numbers. Throughout the stories and verses, illustrations appealing to even the youngest readers attract attention to the role the numbers play.

The storybook section ends with "Friends at Play," in which numbers are the central theme. The words are simple and few enough that the child, aided by the full-page illustrations, can read alone. The increased emphasis on numbers makes this section a natural transition to the workbook that follows.

The workbook contains practice exercises in counting, writing numerals, comparing quantities, and matching numerals to the quantities they represent.

Counting, a basic skill that most introductory books take for granted, gets particular attention. First comes instruction in the numbers one through five, and zero; the numbers six through ten are taught later. It is common for young children to count out of order, count some things twice and ignore others completely. As a remedy, they are encouraged here to touch the pictures as they count.

The instructions for writing numerals emphasize consistency. Learning the numeral 9, for example, the child is taught to start at the top, make a circle, and continue downward, to the right of the circle. Once established, this pattern will help children overcome their tendency to reverse numerals.

To broaden the child's understanding of what numbers mean, the workbook stresses practice in matching like quantities of unlike things— such as one door matching one gingerbread house. Once the child can make this abstraction—using numbers independently of the objects being counted—he or she learns to put the appropriate numeral in writing.

The workbook closes with "Games and Puzzles," based on the stories and rhymes. By helping Hansel and Gretel find the shortest way home, for example, the child uses newly learned skills and has fun in the process.

CONTENTS

THE FIRST STORYBOOK
OF NUMBERS

HANSEL AND GRETEL

Near a great forest in a little cottage there lived long ago a poor woodcutter and his wife, who was stepmother to his 2 children. The boy was named Hansel, and the girl was named Gretel. The family of 4 was very poor indeed. They had scarcely enough bread and porridge to eat.

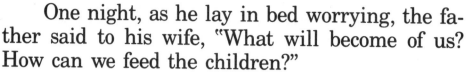

One night, as he lay in bed worrying, the father said to his wife, "What will become of us? How can we feed the children?"

"I'll tell you what, husband," said the woman. "Tomorrow we must take the children into the woods and lose them. Then we shall be rid of them and not have to worry about feeding them."

The poor children had not been able to sleep because they were so hungry. When they heard this, Gretel began to cry.

"Don't worry, Gretel," whispered Hansel. "I have an idea."

When all was quiet he put on his coat and slipped out. The moon was shining bright above, and the little white stones that lay around the house shone like pieces of silver. Hansel filled the pockets of his coat with 10 stones.

As the sun was rising the next morning the stepmother woke Hansel and Gretel. "Get up, lazybones," she said. "We are going into the woods. Here are 4 pieces of bread for your dinner."

The family started off into the forest. Hansel kept behind the others, 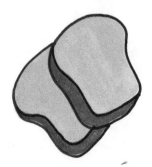 and only Gretel saw him every now and then take a stone from his pocket and drop it onto the ground. When they were deep in the forest their father built a fire.

"You stay here and rest," the stepmother said to the children. "When we are ready we will fetch you." Hansel and Gretel sat by the fire. At noon they ate the 4 pieces of bread. Then their eyes grew tired and they fell asleep. When they awoke it was night, and Gretel began to cry.

"Wait until the moon rises," said Hansel. "Then we can follow the shining white pebbles home."

When the moon rose, the white pebbles shone like silver and showed them the way home. When they pushed open the door their stepmother said, "You are naughty children to sleep so long in the woods." But their father, who loved them, was glad to see them safe.

Later that night the children heard their stepmother say to their father, "Almost all the food is used up. We have only 1 loaf of bread left. When it is gone we shall have nothing at all to eat. We must take the children deeper into the woods this time so that they will not be able to get back."

The poor man had to give in once more. Again the children were not asleep and heard all the talk. Hansel got out of bed to get more stones, but the stepmother had locked the door. Early the next morning the woman pulled the children out of bed. She gave them only 3 pieces of bread for dinner. On the way into the forest Hansel, having no stones, dropped crumbs of bread on the ground.

Again the stepmother and her husband left the children by a fire, deeper in the woods than they had ever been before. Gretel was frightened but tired. She mumbled sleepily to Hansel, "Let's say our evening prayer."

9

When I lay me down to sleep,
8 angels over me to keep.
2 to stand beside my head,
2 below my little bed,
2 protect me with their wings,
2 wake me when morning sings.
They will lead, should I not rise,
To Heaven's shining Paradise.

After they said their prayer they fell asleep. When they awoke it was night. Alas, at moonrise, they could find no crumbs of bread. A family of 5 birds who lived in the woods had eaten them all. Hansel thought they could find their way home anyway. So they walked all that night and until evening the next day. They

found nothing to eat but 6 berries. When they were too tired to walk another step they laid down under a tree and slept.

The next day as Hansel and Gretel were looking for something to eat, they saw 1 beautiful snow-white bird sitting on a low tree branch singing sweetly. As they drew near the bird, it fluttered away. It was so beautiful and sang so sweetly that they followed it until they came to a little house in the woods.

When they were quite close to the house they saw that it was made of bread. Its roof was made of cake and its 4 windows of clear spun sugar. Hansel counted 7 candy canes built into the walls, and Gretel counted 10 gingerbread boys and girls forming a fence around the house. A path of 8 gumdrops led from the gate in the fence to the door of the house.

12

"This house will make a good meal for us," said a very hungry Hansel. "Try some of this window, Gretel."

As Hansel was tasting a bit of the roof and Gretel licked at a window pane they heard a small voice call from within the house,

"Nibble, nibble, like a mouse,
Who is nibbling at my house?"

Then the door opened and a little old woman came out, leaning on a crutch. Hansel and Gretel were frightened, but the little old woman kindly invited them indoors. She took each child by a hand and led them into her little house.

On a table inside the house a nice big dinner was waiting to be eaten. The children counted 1 big, stuffed roast turkey, 2 pitchers of creamy milk, 3 loaves of fresh bread, 4 pieces of yellow cheese, 5 cupcakes with chocolate frosting, 6 cookies with pink icing, 7 tasty oranges, 8 bright red apples, 9 gumdrops of different colors, and 10 brown nuts.

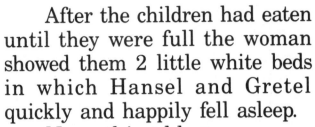

After the children had eaten until they were full the woman showed them 2 little white beds in which Hansel and Gretel quickly and happily fell asleep.

Now, this old woman was really a witch, who liked nothing better than to eat little children. So early in the morning she dragged Hansel out of bed and hurried him off to a little stable, where she locked him behind a barred door. She was going to fatten him up to eat.

Every morning thereafter the old woman hobbled to the stable and cried, "Hansel, put your finger out and let me feel how fat you are." But Hansel knew that the witch could not see well, so he held out a chicken bone instead. The old witch felt the bone and wondered why he did not get fatter.

When many weeks had passed, the witch grew tired of waiting for Hansel to fatten. "Be he fat or be he thin," she cried, "Tomorrow's the day that I'll eat him!"

So the witch made Gretel get up very early the next morning, fill the kettle with water from the well, and make a fire. "First we will bake," the old witch said to Gretel. "Creep inside the oven and tell me if it is hot enough."

"But how am I to get in?" asked Gretel, for she did not want to be roasted.

"Stupid goose!" cried the witch. "The opening is big enough. Look, I could get in myself." To show Gretel how easy it was she stooped and stuck her head and shoulders inside.

14

Quick as a flash, Gretel gave the witch a push, and in she went all the way! Gretel banged the door shut and bolted it. Next she ran as fast as she could to the stable and unlocked the door.

"Hansel!" she cried. "We are free! The old witch is dead!"

Out sprang Hansel, like a bird set free from its cage. As they had nothing more to fear, they went into the witch's house.

In every corner they found chests full of pearls and precious stones.

"These are better than pebbles," said Hansel as he filled his pockets with diamonds and rubies, and Gretel filled her apron with huge pearls.

"Now home we go, if we can find our way out of this enchanted woods."

That proved simple enough, for soon the snow-white bird appeared again and led them back to the familiar path through the woods. They followed the path until they saw their father's house in the distance.

They began to run. They ran straight into their father's arms. He had not had a happy moment since the day he left the children in the woods. And his wife, weary of seeing him shed tears over them, had packed her bags and left.

"See, Father, what we've brought!" shouted the children. Gretel shook her apron and scattered pearls all over the floor. Hansel emptied his pockets, too.

And so all of their troubles were ended, for whenever they needed food they sold 1 of the pearls, or 1 of the rubies, or 1 of the diamonds. They never went to bed without supper again, and they lived happily in the cottage near the forest from that day on.

THE UGLY DUCKLING

The country was lovely. It was summer. In the shade of 5 tall trees that formed a shelter near a farmhouse a duck was sitting on her nest of 6 eggs. Her 6 little ducklings were just about to be hatched.

"About time," thought the mother duck. "I've been sitting on these 6 eggs for such a long time!"

At last 1 egg began to crack. "Cheep! Cheep!" the chick said as he pushed his head through the crack. Soon another egg cracked, and there were now 2 chicks sitting in the nest. Then another came pecking its way out, and then there were 3. Before long they were joined by another

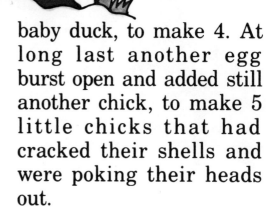

baby duck, to make 4. At long last another egg burst open and added still another chick, to make 5 little chicks that had cracked their shells and were poking their heads out.

"How big the world is!" chirped the 5 young ones. "It is ever so much bigger than the inside of an egg!"

"Do you imagine this is the whole world, my 5 little babies?" said the mother duck. "The world stretches a long way on the other side of the garden, right into the next field. I suppose you are all here now?" she said as she got up. "No, I declare you are not all hatched yet! There is 1 egg still to hatch. The biggest egg is still here. How long is this going to last?" Again the mother duck settled herself on the nest as her 5 little chicks just sat and watched.

"Well, how are you getting on?" asked 2 turkeys who came to pay her a visit.

"This big egg is taking such a long time," answered the mother duck. "The shell will not crack. But now you must look at these 5. They are the finest ducklings I have ever seen. They are all exactly like their father."

"Let us look at the egg that won't crack," said the 2 turkeys. "Why, it looks like a turkey's egg!" they exclaimed. "And we must tell you that turkeys are afraid of water. Why not leave it with us while you teach the other children to swim?"

"No," said the duck, "I have sat so long already that I may as well sit a little while longer."

"Well, good-bye then," said the 2 turkeys as they left the mother duck to sit quietly on the big egg.

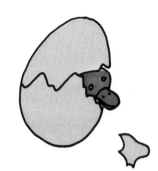

At last, just when the mother duck was about to give up sitting on the big egg, it began to crack. The crack got wider and wider until finally, "Cheep! Cheep!" said a young bird as he tumbled out.

How big and ugly he was! At first the mother duck and the 5 other ducklings just looked at him. "That is certainly a big duckling!" the mother duck said at last. "None of the other 5 look like that. I wonder, can it really be that he is a turkey chick? Well, we shall soon see if he can swim. If he cannot swim then he must be a turkey chick."

So the mother duck led her 6 babies to the pond. Splash! Into the water she went. "Quack, quack!" she commanded and then 1, 2, 3, 4, 5, 6 ducklings jumped in—even the ugly duckling.

"No, that is not a turkey chick," the mother duck said. "See how beautifully he uses his legs to swim and how straight he holds himself. He is indeed my very own chick."

Later, after their swimming lesson, the mother duck took her 6 babies into the barnyard to meet the other animals. The 6 ducklings followed close behind their mother.

In the barnyard the ducklings saw 1 big red rooster, 2 spotted dogs, 3 gray geese, 4 furry cats, 5 fat turkeys, 7 white chickens, and 8 baby chickens. They also saw a family of 9 tiny mice scamper across the barnyard while 10 big black crows sat on the fence, hoping to steal some grain from the food bucket.

The other animals stared at the ducklings and said quite loud, "Just look there! Now we are to have 6 more ducks, just as if there were not enough of us already. They will take up too much space in our yard and, oh dear, how ugly that dark gray duckling is!" And all the animals chased the biggest duckling and bit him in the neck and back.

"You have 5 handsome children," said an old duck. "They are all good looking except the biggest. It's a pity you can't make him over again."

"He is not handsome," said the mother duck, "but he is a good child and he swims as well as any of the others." She patted his neck and stroked his downy feathers.

Soon the 5 little ducklings began to feel quite at home, but the poor ugly duckling was bitten and pushed about and made fun of by the ducks and hens. Even the girl who fed them kicked him aside. No one loved the ugly duckling except his mother. But one day, she became so tired of all the trouble that even she said, "I wish to goodness you were 10 miles away!"

So he ran off as fast as his 2 legs could go. He ran on and on for days until he came to a great marsh, where 7 wild ducks lived. He was so tired and unhappy that he went to sleep immediately. In the morning the 7 wild ducks flew up to meet the visitor. "What sort of bird are you?" they asked. "You are frightfully ugly, but that does not matter to us, as long as you don't want to be friends."

Poor fellow. He knew he was too ugly to have friends. All he wanted was to live among the bushes and drink a little marsh water. He stayed a few days in the marsh, but he was not happy. And so he flew away from the marsh.

Toward night he reached a poor little cottage. It was such a poor house that it could not make up its mind which way to fall and so it remained standing. He saw that the door had fallen off, and a hinge hung so crookedly that he could creep into the house through the crack. Inside the house he saw the old woman who lived there with her 3 cats and her 4 hens. He silently crept into a corner and slept there the whole night.

In the morning the duckling was awakened by a terrible racket. It was the 3 cats meowing and the 4 hens clucking. He ran to see what was happening and was discovered immediately. The 3 cats and 4 hens weren't very friendly, but they let the duckling sit in the corner of the room. But the ugly duckling wasn't very happy just staying inside the cottage and sitting quietly in the corner. Soon he began to think of fresh air and sunshine. Oh, how he wanted to float on the water. At last he could not help telling the 4 hens about it.

"What on earth possesses you?" asked a hen. "You have nothing to do. That is why you get these strange ideas into your head," said another. "Lay some eggs like we do or take to purring like those 3 silly cats and you will get over it."

But the ugly duckling didn't think he would ever learn to lay eggs like a hen or purr like a cat. "I think I will go to see more of the wide world," said the duckling.

"Go ahead," said the 4 hens in disgust. "Please yourself."

So away went the duckling. He floated on the water from place to place, scorned by every other animal because of his ugliness.

Now the autumn came, and one evening, just as the sun was setting, a flock of 10 beautiful large birds appeared out of the bushes. They were 10 dazzling white swans with gracefully curved necks. They uttered a peculiar cry as they spread their broad wings and flew away toward warmer lands and open seas.

The little ugly duckling stretched his neck up into the air after them. Oh, he could not forget those 10 beautiful and happy birds. He did not know what they were but he wanted to be like them more than any other animal he had ever seen.

Winter followed autumn, and it became so terribly cold that the duckling had to swim about in the water to keep from freezing. To stop himself from thinking about how cold it was he would count over and over again, 1, 2, 3, 4, 5, 6, 7, 8, 9, 10 beautiful, happy birds.

But every night the hole in which he swam got smaller. At last he was so weary that he could move no more, and he froze fast into the ice.

Early in the morning a man came along searching for firewood and saw the duckling frozen in the ice. He hammered a hole in the ice with his heavy shoe and carried the duckling home to his wife and 8 children. They placed him by the fire, and soon he was again warm. The children wanted to play with him, but the duckling was so frightened seeing all 8 of them coming toward him that he rushed into the milk pan and spattered milk all over the room. Then he flew into the butter cask and down into the meal tub and out again. Just imagine what he looked like by this time!

The woman screamed and tried to hit him with a broom, and the 8 children tumbled over one another trying to catch him. By good luck the door stood open, and the duckling flew out among the bushes and new fallen snow and lay there. He was so very tired.

The ugly duckling had many other unhappy days, but it would be too sad to tell you of all the hard times he went through during the long, cold winter.

One day, when spring had finally arrived, the duckling was in the marsh, lying among the rushes. He stretched his wings, and they suddenly felt different, much stronger than before. Moving his wings faster and faster, he rose high in the air and flew away.

Before he knew what had happened he found himself in a large garden with a lovely lake. Just in front of him he saw 3 beautiful swans with white, rustling feathers. They swam lightly over the water. The duckling remembered seeing the beautiful white birds and suddenly felt a strange sadness.

"I will fly up to the lovely swans, and they will bite me because I am so ugly. Better to be killed by them than snapped at by ducks and pecked at by all."

So he flew into the water and swam toward the swans. They saw him and darted toward him with ruffled feathers. "Kill me, oh kill me!" said the poor duckling, bowing his head.

Reflected in the water he saw the image of a graceful swan. "I'm not a duck after all!" he exclaimed. "I'm a swan, as beautiful as any." The other swans swam swiftly toward him, and welcomed him to their pond.

Soon 2 little children came into the garden. Each child had 1 piece of bread and 9 pieces of corn, which they threw into the water. The smallest child cried out, "There is a new one!" and the children clapped their hands and danced around their newest friend.

The new swan felt so shy that he hid his head under his wing. Now, as he heard them say he was the most beautiful of all beautiful birds, he remembered how badly he had been treated before. Gradually, as he heard them praise his beauty again and again, he realized his unhappy days were over at last. Proudly raising his head, and extending his wings, he said with gladness in his heart, "I never dreamt of such happiness when I was only an ugly duckling."

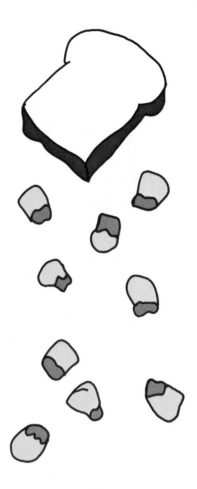

JACK AND THE BEANSTALK

A long, long time ago there lived a small family of 3 people—1 father, 1 mother, and 1 son named Jack. Jack was their only child and he was a dreamer. His father was ill and could not work. His mother was busy from early morning to late at night working and planning how to support her sick husband and her son.

The family did own 1 cow, Milky White, which gave them milk and butter to sell. They also owned some fruit trees. There were 2 apple trees, 2 pear trees, and 2 peach trees, but these gave fruit only in the summer. When winter came, the trees of the field hid from the frost and the winds, and there was very little food to eat.

Though his mother sent Jack to gather what food he could find, he came back as often as not with a very empty sack, for Jack's eyes were so often full of wonder at all the things he saw that sometimes he forgot to look for food.

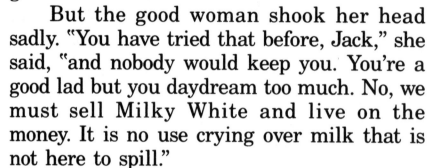

So it came to pass one morning that Milky White gave almost no milk—only 3 bucketfuls. The 3 buckets of milk would barely feed the family, and there would be none left to sell.

Jack's mother threw her apron over her head and sobbed, "What shall we do? What shall we do?"

Now Jack, who loved his mother, was very sorry that he did so little to help. So he said, "Cheer up! Cheer up! I will get work somewhere. I will work my fingers to the bone."

But the good woman shook her head sadly. "You have tried that before, Jack," she said, "and nobody would keep you. You're a good lad but you daydream too much. No, we must sell Milky White and live on the money. It is no use crying over milk that is not here to spill."

"Just so," he cried. "We will sell Milky White and be richer than ever. On market day I will take her to town, and we shall see what money she will bring."

"But," began his mother.

" 'But' doesn't butter parsnips," laughed Jack. "Trust me to make a good bargain."

Since market day happened also to be washing day, and her husband was sicker than usual, his mother let Jack set off to sell the cow on his own.

"Not less than 4 dollars!" she cried after him as he turned the corner.

"Hrmph, 4 dollars, indeed," thought Jack. He had made up his mind to get much more than 4 dollars.

He was just deciding what gift he should buy for his mother with some of the money when he saw 4 strange little old men on the road who called out, "Good morning, Jack."

There on the road were 4 little men with 4 big hats and 4 tiny umbrellas, smoking 4 of the longest pipes you have ever seen.

"Good morning," replied Jack with a polite bow and wondering how the 4 strange little old men happened to know his name, though to be sure, Jacks were as plentiful as blackberries.

"And where may you be going?" asked the 4.

Jack wondered what the 4 strange little old men had to do with him, but being always polite he replied, "I'm going to market to sell Milky White and I mean to make a good bargain."

"So you will, so you will," chuckled the 4 strange little old men. "You look the sort of chap for it. We'll bet you know how many beans make 5."

"Why, 2 in each hand and 1 in my mouth, of course," answered Jack readily. He really was sharp as a needle. "I know all about 5. I have 5 fingers on this hand and 5 again on the other. I also have 5 toes on this foot and 5 again on the other."

"Just so, just so," chuckled the strange little old men, and as they talked they gave Jack 5 beans. "Well, here they are, so give us Milky White."

Jack was so surprised that he stood with his mouth open as if he expected the 5 beans to fly into it. "What?" he said at last. "My Milky White for 5 common beans? Not if I can help it!"

"But these 5 aren't common beans," replied the strange little old men, and there was a strange little smile on each strange little face. "If you plant these beans tonight, by the morning they will have grown up into the sky."

Jack was too surprised this time even to open his mouth, and his eyes opened instead. "Did you say right up into the very sky?" he asked at last. You see, Jack had wondered more about the sky than anything else.

"Right up into the very sky," repeated the strange little old men with a nod between each word. "It's a good bargain, Jack, and if you don't agree you shall have Milky White back again. Will that please you?"

"Right as rain," cried Jack without stopping to think and the next moment he found himself standing alone in the road. "5 is 2 in each hand and 1 in my mouth," repeated Jack. "That is what I said and what I'll do. Everything in order, and if what the strange little old men said isn't true I shall get Milky White back tomorrow morning." So whistling and munching 1 bean, he cheerfully started for home, wondering what the sky would be like if he ever got there.

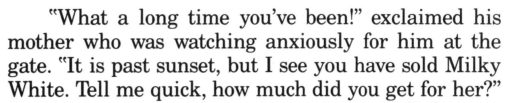

"What a long time you've been!" exclaimed his mother who was watching anxiously for him at the gate. "It is past sunset, but I see you have sold Milky White. Tell me quick, how much did you get for her?"

"You'll never guess," began Jack.

"Don't tease me," said the good woman. "I have worried about you all day, afraid that you might have been tricked. How much did you get? At least 4 dollars I hope. Could it be 5 dollars?"

Jack triumphantly held out his hand and showed her 4 beans. "There," he said, "that's what I got for her, and 1 more just like them. I got 5 beans for Milky White. A jolly good bargain, too. These are much more valuable than 5 dollars."

"What!" she said. "Only 5 beans?"

"Yes," replied Jack, beginning to doubt his own wisdom, "but these are magic beans. If you plant them tonight, by morning they will have grown up into the sky."

But Jack's mother wasn't listening, for she had lost her temper and was hitting poor Jack. When she had finished scolding and beating him she flung the 4 miserable beans out of the window into the garden and sent him to bed without supper.

"If this is the magical effect of the beans," thought Jack, "I don't want any more magic, if you please!" And soon he forgot all about the beans and fell fast asleep.

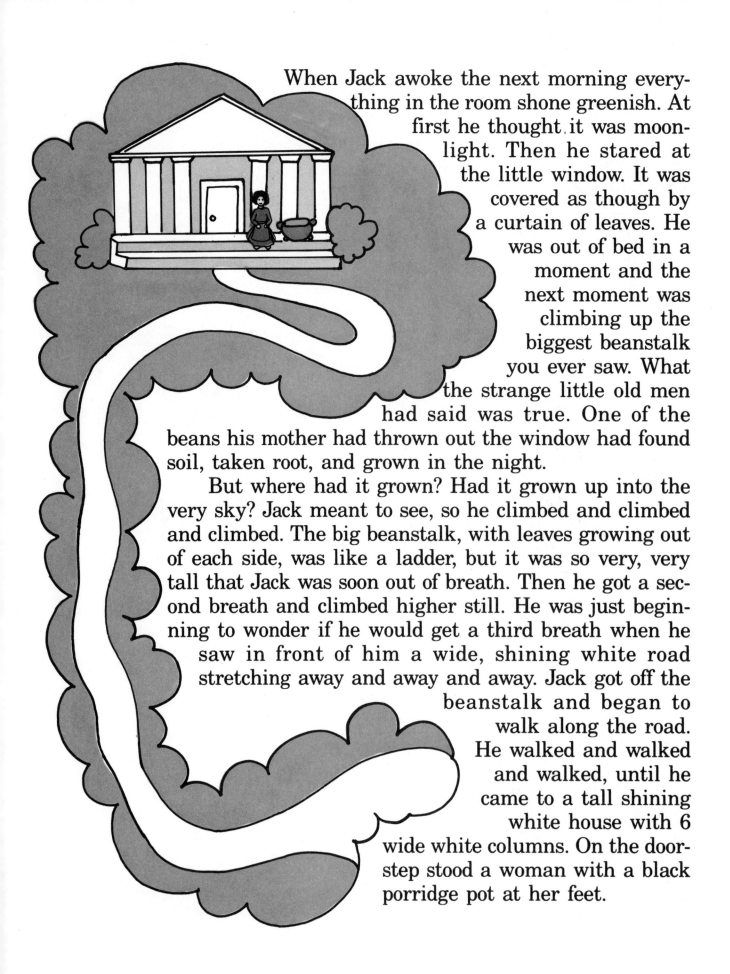

When Jack awoke the next morning everything in the room shone greenish. At first he thought it was moonlight. Then he stared at the little window. It was covered as though by a curtain of leaves. He was out of bed in a moment and the next moment was climbing up the biggest beanstalk you ever saw. What the strange little old men had said was true. One of the beans his mother had thrown out the window had found soil, taken root, and grown in the night.

But where had it grown? Had it grown up into the very sky? Jack meant to see, so he climbed and climbed and climbed. The big beanstalk, with leaves growing out of each side, was like a ladder, but it was so very, very tall that Jack was soon out of breath. Then he got a second breath and climbed higher still. He was just beginning to wonder if he would get a third breath when he saw in front of him a wide, shining white road stretching away and away and away. Jack got off the beanstalk and began to walk along the road. He walked and walked and walked, until he came to a tall shining white house with 6 wide white columns. On the doorstep stood a woman with a black porridge pot at her feet.

Now Jack, having had no supper, was as hungry as a hunter. When he saw the porridge pot he said quite politely, "Good morning, madam. I wonder if you could give me some breakfast?"

"Breakfast?" echoed the woman who in truth was an ogre's wife. "If it's breakfast you're wanting, it's breakfast you'll likely be, for I expect my man home any minute and there's nothing he likes better for breakfast than a boy—a fat boy grilled on toast!"

Jack wasn't at all a coward, and when he wanted a thing he generally got it. So he said very cheerfully, "I'd be fatter if I ate some of that porridge.

The ogre's wife laughed and told Jack to come in, for she wasn't really half as bad as she looked.

As soon as he had finished 6 great big bowls of porridge and 6 eggs and 6 glasses of milk, the house began to tremble and quake. It was the ogre coming home. Thump, thump, THUMP!

"Into the oven with you, sharp!" cried the ogre's wife and the iron oven door was closed just as the ogre strode in. Jack could see him through the little peephole at the top of the oven, where the steam came out. He was a big one for sure and had 7 sheep strung to his belt. These he threw down on the table.

"Here, wife," he cried, "roast me these 7 morsels for breakfast. They're all I've been able to get this morning. The worst luck! I hope the oven is hot." And when he went to touch the handle Jack burst into a sweat, wondering what would happen next.

"Roast?" echoed the ogre's wife. "Pooh, these 7 little things would dry up into cinders. Better to boil them." So she set to work to boil the 7, but the ogre began sniffing around the room.

"They don't smell like mutton meat," he growled. Then he frowned horribly and began this frightening rhyme:
"Fee, fi, fo, fum,
I smell the blood of an Englishman.
Be he alive or be he dead,
I'll grind his bones to make my bread."

"Don't be silly," said the wife. "It's the bones of the 7 little boys you had for supper and I'm boiling down for soup. Come eat your breakfast. That's a good ogre."

So the ogre ate the 7 sheep. When he was done he went to a big oaken chest and took out 8 bags of gold pieces. Jack couldn't believe his eyes. He had never seen 8 bags of gold before. The ogre put the bags on the table and began to count their contents while his wife cleared away the breakfast things. By and by his head began to nod, and at last the ogre began to snore. He snored so loud that the house shook.

Then Jack sneaked out of the oven, seized the 8 bags of gold, and crept away. He ran along the wide, shining white road as fast as his legs would carry him until he came to the beanstalk. He couldn't climb down with the bags of gold, because they were too heavy. So he flung the 8 bags down first and helter skelter scrambled after them. When he came to the bottom, there was his mother, picking up the 8 bags of gold out of the garden as fast as she could.

"Mercy me," she said. "Wherever have you been? See, it's been raining gold!"

"No it hasn't. I climbed up … ," began Jack, turning to look at the beanstalk. But lo and behold, it wasn't there any more! He knew then that the beans really were magic.

For a long time after that they lived happily, spending the ogre's gold to buy many good things to eat.

Then at last the day came when Jack's mother put 1 gold piece into Jack's hand and told him to be very careful when marketing. She told Jack there was no more gold in any of the bags. Now they would surely starve.

That night Jack went to bed without supper. As he was falling asleep he thought what a shame for such a big boy to stuff himself and bring no bread to the table. If he couldn't make money, he decided, he could at any rate eat less food. And so Jack slept.

When he awoke in the morning the whole room shone greenish, and there again was a curtain of leaves over the window. Another bean had grown in the night and Jack was up the stalk like a lamplighter before you could say "night." This time he climbed quickly and it wasn't long before he reached the wide, shining white road. In a second he was standing before the tall white house, where on the wide white steps the ogre's wife was standing with the black porridge pot at her feet and a plate with 8 muffins in her hands.

This time Jack was bold as brass. "Good morning, madam," he said. "I've come to ask you for breakfast, for I've had no supper and I'm as hungry as a hunter. I'd love to gobble up those 8 muffins."

"Go away, bad boy," replied the ogre's wife. "The last time I gave a boy breakfast my man missed all his gold. I believe you are the same boy!"

"Maybe I am, maybe I'm not," said Jack with a laugh. "I'll tell you true when I've had my breakfast, but not until then."

"I can't give you these muffins" cried the woman. But Jack begged and begged and at last the ogre's wife, who was very curious, gave him 8 big bowls of porridge and the 8 muffins, too. But before he had finished he heard the ogre coming.

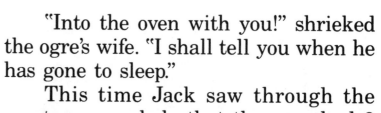

"Into the oven with you!" shrieked the ogre's wife. "I shall tell you when he has gone to sleep."

This time Jack saw through the steam peephole that the ogre had 9 fat calves strung to his belt.

"Better luck today, wife," he cried, and his voice shook the house.

"Quick, roast these 9 trifles for my breakfast. I hope the oven is hot."

As he went to feel the handle of the oven door the wife cried out sharply, "Roast! Why you will have to wait hours before they're done. I'll broil them instead. See how bright the fire is."

"Hrmph," growled the ogre and then began to sniff and call out,

"Fee, fi, fo, fum,
I smell the blood
of an Englishman."

"Twaddle!" said the ogre's wife. "It's only the bones of the 9 boys you had last week and I put into the pig bucket."

"Hrmph!" said the ogre harshly as he ate the 9 broiled calves. Then he said to his wife, "Bring me my hen that lays magic eggs. I want to see gold."

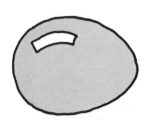

Then the ogre said to the hen, "Lay!" and it promptly laid— what do you think?—1 beautiful, shiny, yellow golden egg! "I shall never have to beg as long as I have you." Then he said, "Lay!" once more and lo and behold there were now 2 beautiful, shiny, yellow golden eggs.

"I want another!" he screamed and the hen obeyed. Now there were 3 eggs. "More!" commanded the ogre and then there were 4 eggs. "4 is not enough!" The hen laid another, to make 5. "Don't stop!" shouted the ogre, and soon there were 6, then 7, then 8, then 9, and finally 10 beautiful, shiny, yellow golden eggs.

Jack could hardly believe his eyes. He made up his mind that he would have that hen, come what may.

When the ogre began to doze, Jack jumped like a flash out of the oven, seized the hen, and ran for his life. But the hen set up such a terrible cackle that it woke the ogre.

"Where's my hen?" he shouted to his wife, and they both rushed to the door. But Jack had a good start on them and all they could see was a little figure running down the wide, shining white road holding a big fluttering black hen by its legs.

How Jack got down the beanstalk he never quite knew. All he remembered was feathers and leaves and feathers and cackling, but get down he did. And waiting on the ground was his mother. She counted 9 black feathers as they fluttered down, and thinking they were bits of a thun-  dercloud began to fear that the sky was going to fall.

The very moment Jack touched ground he called out, "Lay!" and the big black hen laid a great big, shiny, yellow golden egg.

From that moment on, the family had everything that money could buy, for whenever they wanted anything they just said, "Lay!" and the black hen provided them with gold.

Then came a day when Jack began to wonder if he could find something else in the sky besides money. One, fine, moonlit, midsummer night he refused his supper and before going to bed stole out to the garden with a big watering can and watered the ground under his window. "There must be 2 more beans somewhere," he thought. "Perhaps it has been too dry for them to grow." Soon he fell fast asleep.

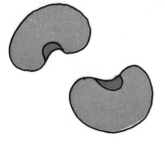

Lo and behold, when he awoke the next morning, there was a greenish light shimmering throughout his room. In an instant he was on the beanstalk climbing, climbing, and climbing, until he reached the wide, shining white road.

This time Jack knew better than to ask for his breakfast, for the ogre's wife would be sure to recognize him. So he hid in some bushes beside the great white house until he saw her in the kitchen. He slipped out and hid in a pot, for he knew she would be sure to look in the oven first thing.

After a little while he heard thump, thump, THUMP! Peeping through a crack in the pot's lid he saw the ogre stalk in with 10 ducks strung to his belt. This time, no sooner had the ogre gotten into the house when he began shouting,

"Fee, fi, fo, fum,
I smell the blood of an Englishman.
Be he alive or be he dead,
I'll grind his bones to make my bread!"

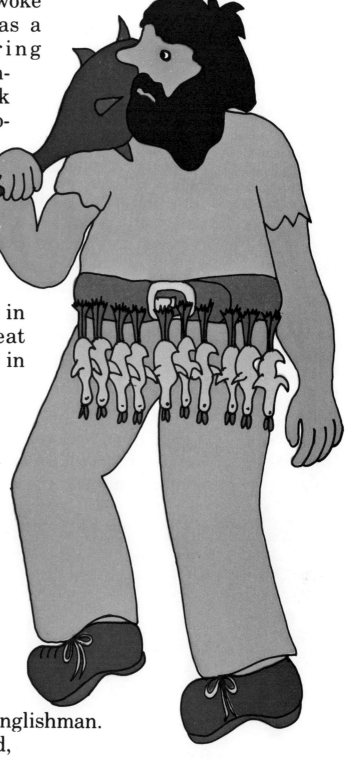

"Well, I declare, so do I!" exclaimed the ogre's wife. "It must be that horrid boy that stole the bags of gold and the hen. If so, he's hiding in the oven."

But when she opened the door there was no Jack, only some joints of meat roasting and sizzling away. She laughed and said, "You and I are fools for sure. Why, it's those boys you caught last night and I am getting ready for your breakfast. Yes, we are fools to take dead meat for live boy. So eat your breakfast. That's a good ogre. Those boys should taste very good to you."

The ogre still wasn't satisfied. Every now and then he would cry out,

"Fee, fi, fo, fum
I smell the blood of an Englishman!"

Then he would get up and search the cupboards, keeping Jack in a fever of fear lest the ogre should think of the pot. But the ogre didn't, and when he had finished his breakfast he called out to his wife, "Bring me my magic harp with the 10 silver strings. I want to be amused."

So he brought out a little harp and put it on the table. The ogre sat back in his chair and said lazily, "Sing." Lo and behold, the harp began to sing. It sang about many things, and it sang so beautifully that Jack forgot to be frightened. The ogre forgot to think of "Fee, fi, fo, fum," and soon fell asleep, forgetting even to snore.

Jack stole out of the pot quiet as a mouse and crept on hands and knees to the table where he raised himself ever so softly. He took hold of the magic harp, which he was determined to have, but no sooner had he touched it than it cried out loud, "Master! Master!"

The ogre awoke, saw Jack making off with the harp, and rushed after him. My goodness, but it was a close race! Jack was nimble, but the ogre's stride was twice as long. Jack raced and jumped and leaped like a rabbit, but when he reached the beanstalk, the ogre was very close behind him.

Jack jumped onto the beanstalk and started down as fast as he could, clutching the harp as it called, "Master! Master!" at the top of its voice. Jack was only about a quarter of the way down the beanstalk when it gave the most terrific lurch and nearly knocked Jack off. It was the ogre beginning to climb down, and his weight made the stalk sway like a tree in a storm. Jack knew then it was life or death, so he climbed down faster and faster, and as he climbed, he shouted, "Mother! Mother! Bring an ax! Bring an ax!"

Jack's mother came running from the backyard, where she was chopping wood, certain that this time the sky really must be falling. Just then Jack touched ground and the harp began singing beautiful things. Jack seized the ax and gave 10 great chops to the beanstalk. With each chop a giant green leaf fell from the beanstalk, which shook and swayed and bent like barley before a breeze.

"Mind your manners, you nasty boy, or I'll have you for supper!" shouted the ogre, clinging to the beanstalk as tight as he could.

But Jack would not stop. He gave the beanstalk another sharp blow, and the ogre and the beanstalk and all came tumbling down. The ogre fell so hard that he died on the spot!

After that, everyone was truly happy, for they had all the gold they needed. If the sick father was sad, Jack just brought out the harp and said, "Sing," and lo and behold, it would sing. Because the harp sang about so many wonderful things, Jack stopped dreaming and wondering so much and became quite a useful person.

But remember this: the 4 strange, little old men gave Jack 5 magic beans. Jack ate 1, and 3 grew into giant beanstalks. The last 1 of Jack's 5 magic beans hasn't grown yet. It's still in the garden. And so, this story isn't really over, and won't be, until some little child climbs that last giant beanstalk into the sky.

44

Nursery Rhymes and Poems

OVER IN THE MEADOW

Over in the meadow in the sand in the sun
Lived an old mother turtle and her little turtle

1

"Dig," said the mother. "We dig," said the 1,
So they dug all day in the sand in the sun.

Over in the meadow where the stream runs blue
Lived an old mother fish and her little fishes

2

"Swim," said the mother. "We swim," said the two,
So they swam all day where the stream runs blue.

Over in the meadow in a hole in a tree
Lived an old mother owl and her little owls

3

"Tu-whoo," said the mother. "Tu-whoo," said the 3,
So they tu-whooed all day in a hole in the tree.

Over in the meadow by the old barn door
Lived an old mother rat and her little ratties

4

"Gnaw," said the mother. "We gnaw," said the 4,
So they gnawed all day by the old barn door.

Over in the meadow in a snug beehive
Lived an old mother bee and her little bees

5

"Buzz," said the mother. "We buzz," said the 5,
So they buzzed all day in a snug beehive.

Over in the meadow in a nest built of sticks
Lived an old mother crow and her little crows

6

"Caw," said the mother. "We caw," said the 6,
So they cawed all day in a nest built of sticks.

Over in the meadow where the grass grows so even
Lived an old mother frog and her little froggies

"Jump," said the mother. "We jump," said the 7,
So they jumped all day where the grass grows so even.

Over in the meadow by the old mossy gate
Lived an old mother lizard and her little lizards

8

"Bask," said the mother. "We bask," said the 8,
So they basked all day by the old mossy gate.

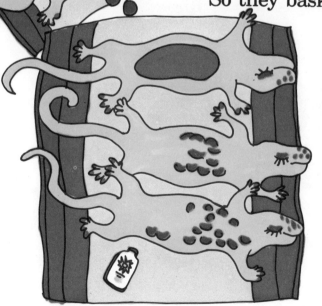

8

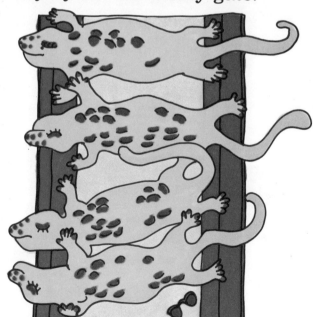

Over in the meadow by the old scotch pine
Lived an old mother duck and her little ducks

"Quack," said the mother. "We quack," said the 9,
So they quacked all day by the old scotch pine.

Over in the meadow in a cozy wee den
Lived an old mother beaver and her little beavers

10

"Beave," said the mother. "We beave," said the 10,
So they beaved all day in a cozy wee den.

10 LITTLE INDIANS

10 little Indians
Standing in a line,
1 toddled home,
And then there were 9.

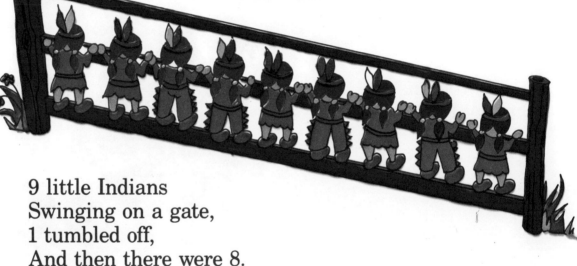

9 little Indians
Swinging on a gate,
1 tumbled off,
And then there were 8.

8 little Indians
Never heard of heaven,
1 went to sleep,
And then there were 7.

7 little Indians
Built a fire of sticks,
1 burnt his finger,
and then there were 6.

6 little Indians
Dipping honey from a hive,
1 got stung,
And then there were 5.

5 little Indians
On a cellar door,
1 tumbled in,
And then there were 4.

4 little Indians
Out on a spree,
1 got sick,
And then there were 3.

3 little Indians
Out in a canoe,
1 slipped overboard,
And then there were 2.

2 little Indians
Running in the sun,
1 stopped to rest,
And then there was 1.

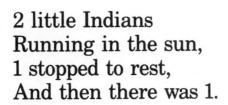

1 little Indian
Tired from all the fun,
Went home to bed,
And then there was none.

OLD KING COLE

Old King Cole was a merry old soul,
And a merry old soul was he.
He called for his pipe, and he called for his bowl,
And he called for his fiddlers 3.

Every fiddler, he had a fiddle,
And the fiddle went tweedle-dee.
Oh, there's none so rare as can compare
With King Cole and his fiddlers 3.

Then he called for his fifers 2,
And they puffed and they blew tootle-oo;
And King Cole laughed as his glass he quaffed,
And his fifers puffed tootle-oo.

Then he called for 1 drummer boy,
The army's pride and joy.
And the thuds out-rang with a loud bang! bang!
The noise of the noisiest toy.

Then he called for his trumpeters 4,
Who stood at his own palace door,
And they played trang-a-trang
Whilst the drummer went bang,
And King Cole called for more.

He called for a man to conduct,
Who into his bed had been tuck'd,
And he had to get up without bite or sup
And waggle his stick and conduct.

Old King Cole laughed with glee,
Such rare antics to see.
There never was a man in merry England
Who was half as merry as he.

THE END

When I was 1,
I had just begun.

When I was 2,
I was nearly new.

When I was 3,
I was hardly me.

When I was 4,
I was not much more.

When I was 5,
I was just alive.

But now I'm 6, I'm as clever as clever;
So I think I'll be 6 now for ever and ever.

by A. A. Milne

56

MAGPIE CHATTER

I saw 8 magpies in a tree,
2 for you and 6 for me:
  1 for sorrow,
  2 for mirth,
  3 for a wedding,
  4 for a birth,
  5 for England,
  6 for France,
  7 for a fiddler,
  8 for a dance.

A FISHY STORY

1, 2, 3, 4, 5,
Once I caught a fish alive.
Why did you let it go?
Because it bit my fingers so.

6, 7, 8, 9, 10,
Shall we go to fish again?
Not today, some other time,
For I have broke my fishing line.

RHYMES RIDDLED WITH NUMBERS

The 1st little pig went to market,

The 2nd little pig stayed home,

The 3rd little pig had roast beef,

The 4th little pig had none,

And the 5th little pig cried
wee, wee, wee
All the way home.

RHYMES RIDDLED WITH NUMBERS

3 young rats with black felt hats,
3 young ducks with white straw flats,
3 young dogs with curling tails,
3 young cats with demi veils
Went out to walk with 2 young pigs
In satin vests and sorrel wigs;
But suddenly it chanced to rain,
And so they all went home again.

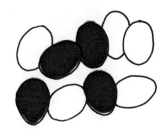

Hickety, Pickety, my black hen,
She lays eggs for gentlemen;
Sometimes 9, sometimes 10,
Hickety, Pickety, my black hen.

3 blind mice, see how they run!
They all ran after the farmer's wife,
Who cut off their tails with a carving knife.
Did you ever see such a thing in your life
As 3 blind mice?

TWIDDLE A RIDDLE

3 large ladies heard it thunder.
3 large ladies all got under
1 small umbrella, or tried to get.
Why didn't the 3 large ladies get wet?

It didn't rain.

I know that you've heard alarms
Of many queer things;
But what has 8 legs, 2 arms,
3 heads, and wings?

A man on horseback
with a canary
on his head.

FIVE LITTLE SISTERS

5 little sisters walking in a row;
Now isn't that the best way for little girls to go?
Each had a round hat, each had a muff,
And each had a new pelisse of soft green stuff.

5 little marigolds standing in a row;
Now, isn't that the best way for marigolds to grow?
Each with a green stalk, and all the 5 had got
A bright yellow flower and a new red pot.

by Kate Greenaway

BAA, BAA, BLACK SHEEP

Baa, baa, black sheep,
Have you any wool?
Yes, sir, yes, sir,
3 bags full;

1 for my master,
1 for my dame,
1 for the little boy
Who lives down the lane.

A CAT TALE

5 little pussy cats sitting in a row,
Blue ribbons 'round each neck,
Fastened in a bow.
Hey, pussies! Ho, pussies! Are your faces clean?
Don't you know you're sitting
There so as to be seen?

Friends at Play

When I wake up in the morning there is only 1 person in my bed—ME!

2 people can talk on the telephone for hours.

3 of us play house.

4 boys fly kites on a windy day.

Happiness +
is
Home Made

5 makes a perfect tea party.

With 6 you can play school.

7 boys and girls play music together.

8 children see who can swing the highest.

9 is enough to start a ballgame.

10 friends with hats and horns—
it must be someone's birthday party.

1 boy needs 1 bed.

2 people need 2 telephones.

3 friends need 3 hats.

4 boys need 4 kites.

5 friends need 5 cups of tea.

6 school children need 6 pencils.

7 musicians need 7 horns.

8 children need 8 swings.

9 ballplayers need 9 uniforms.

10 partygoers need 10 pieces of cake.

FIRST WORKBOOK
OF NUMBERS

Practicing Together

Let's count gingerbread cookies. Count aloud.

As you count aloud, touch each cookie. Remember to say only one number for each cookie you touch.

Touch and count.

Touch and count.

Touch and count.

Practicing Together

Let's count little Indians. Count aloud.

As you count aloud, touch each Indian. Remember to say only one number for each little Indian you touch.

Touch and count.

Touch and count.

Touch and count.

Now It's Your Turn

Count the beautiful swans. Count aloud.

Start at the left and move to the right. Remember to say only one number for each swan you touch.

Touch and count.

Touch and count.

Touch and count.

Now It's Your Turn

Count the little pigs.

Remember to say only one number for each pig you touch. Start at the left and move to the right.

Touch and count.

Touch and count.

Touch and count.

Practicing Together

Let's match numbers.

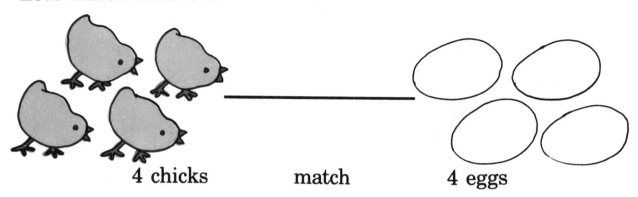

4 chicks   match   4 eggs

There is the same number of eggs as chicks. No matter how different they look, we can say they match in number. Because they match in number, we draw a line between them.

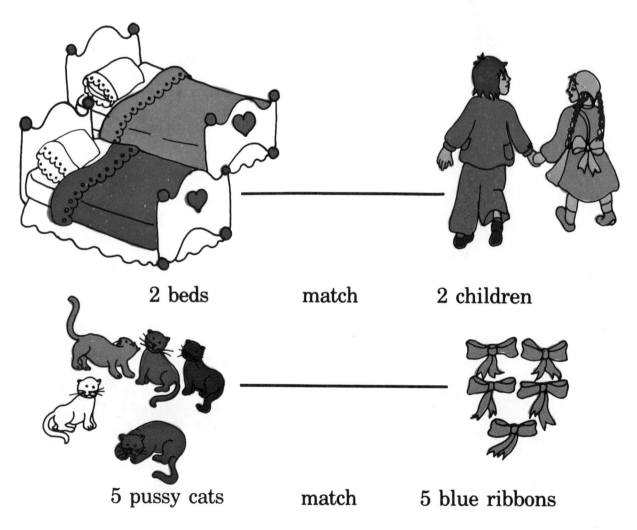

2 beds   match   2 children

5 pussy cats   match   5 blue ribbons

Now It's Your Turn

Let's match numbers.

4 umbrellas

4 pipes

Draw lines between the groups that match in number.

2 fish

2 pigs

1 duckling

1 pond

3 men

3 fiddles

Stop and Look

See how they match.

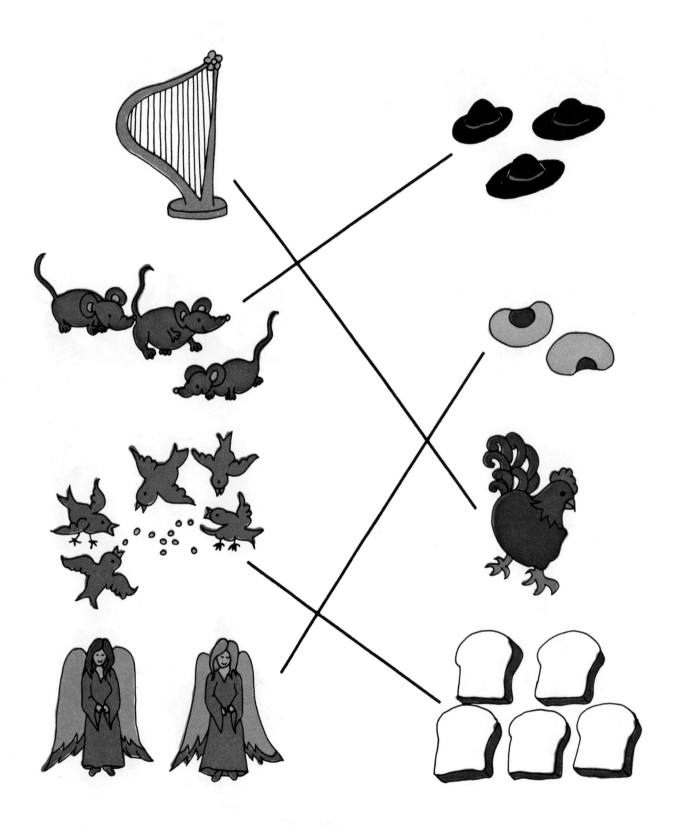

Now It's Your Turn

Draw lines between the groups that match in number.

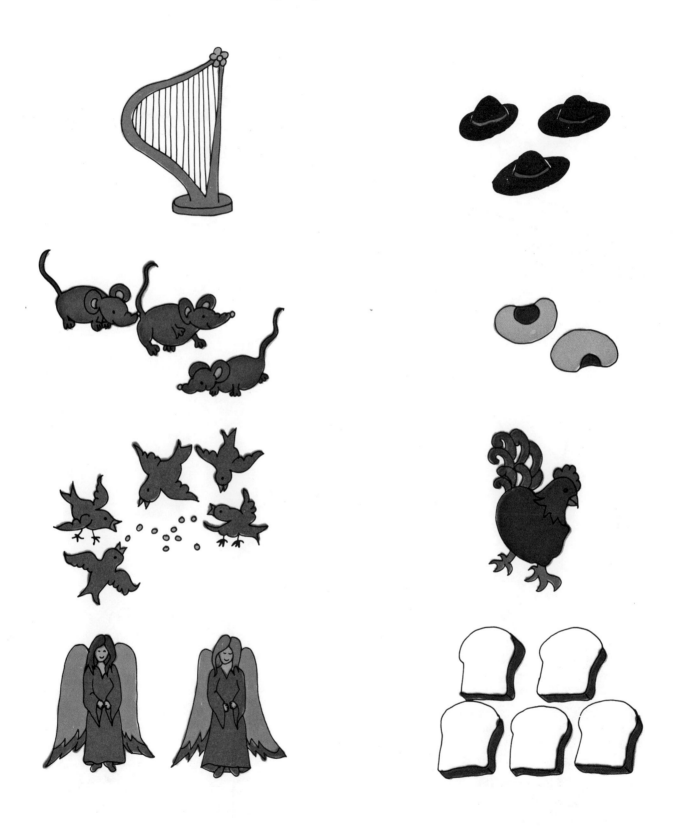

Stop and Look

Lines and circles are everywhere.

Now It's Your Turn

Practice writing lines. Always start at the top.

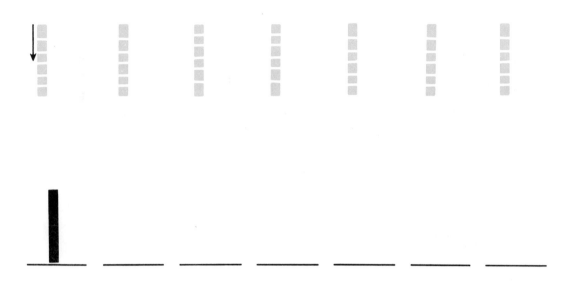

Which line looks the best?

Practice writing circles. Start at the top and move to the left.

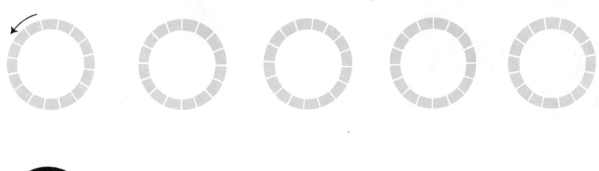

Which circle looks the best?

Stop and Look

Now It's Your Turn

Practice writing numerals 1 and 2.

Trace these numerals. Always start at the top.

Write a numeral 1 on each line. Then pick out your best 1.

Trace these numerals. Remember to start at the top.

2 _____ _____ _____ _____ _____ _____ _____

Write a numeral 2 on each line. Which 2 looks the best?

Stop and Look

Now It's Your Turn

Practice writing numerals 3 and 4.

Trace these numerals. Always start at the top.

3 _ _ _ _ _ _

Write a numeral 3 on each line. Which 3 looks the best?

Trace these numerals. Start at the top.

4 _ _ _ _ _ _

Write a numeral 4 in each space. Which 4 looks the best?

Stop and Look

Can you count the fingers on your hand?

Can you hop 5 times on your left foot?

98

Now It's Your Turn

Practice writing the numeral 5.

↓1 5 →5 5 5 5 5

Trace these numerals. Start at the top.

5 ___ ___ ___ ___ ___

Write a numeral 5 on each line. Which 5 looks best?

Do you remember how to trace these numerals?

___ ___ ___ ___

Now write the numerals 1 through 5.

Stop and Look

Count the boxes in each row.

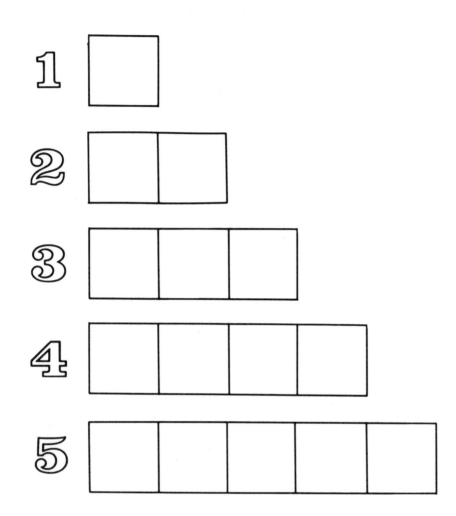

Can you see that each row has one more box than the
row above it?

Which row has more boxes than any other row?

Did you pick the row with 5 boxes? This row has the
most boxes.

Now It's Your Turn

Color the number of boxes in each row to match the numeral.

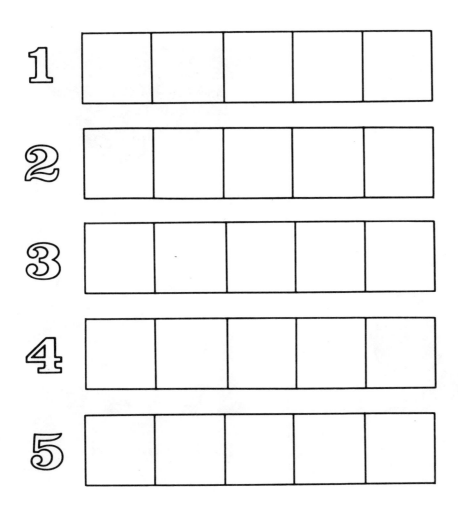

Each row should have one more colored box than the row above it.

Did you color one more box in each row?

Did you color all the boxes in the last row?

Practicing Together

Touch and count.

1 rooster

1 loaf of bread

2 apple trees

2 little Indians

3 gray geese

3 buckets of milk

Now It's Your Turn

Touch, count, and write the correct numeral in each box.

How many
roosters? ☐

How many
loaves of bread? ☐

How many
apple trees? ☐

How many
little Indians? ☐

How many
gray geese? ☐

How many
buckets of milk? ☐

Practicing Together

Touch and count.

5 gingerbread cookies

3 beautiful swans

4 angels

5 birds

3 young dogs

4 pieces of cheese

Now It's Your Turn

Touch, count, and write the correct numeral in each box.

How many
gingerbread cookies? ☐

How many
beautiful swans? ☐

How many
angels? ☐

How many
birds? ☐

How many
young dogs? ☐

How many
pieces of cheese? ☐

Can you find these:

1 duckling   2 turkeys   3 swans   4 cats   5 trees

Now It's Your Turn

Touch, count, and draw lines to the matching numerals.

Stop and Look

Here is a story about the number ZERO.

One day Gretel had
5 gingerbread cookies.

She ate a cookie, and then
there were **4**.

She ate another, and then
there were **3**.

She gave one to Hansel, and then
there were **2**.

She dropped one, and then
there was **1**.

She gave her last cookie to a hungry dog, and then
there was **0**.

Now It's Your Turn

Can you answer this question?

How many red hens are in this box?

The answer is none. The box is empty!

There is a special numeral that means none. It is called zero, and it looks like a circle: 0.

Practice writing the numeral 0.

Remember to start at the top. Then move to the left.

Which numeral 0 looks the best?

Practicing Together

Let's count bright red apples.

Count aloud as you touch each apple. Remember to say only one number for each apple you touch.

Touch and count.

Touch and count.

Touch and count.

Practicing Together

Let's count golden eggs. Count aloud.

As you count aloud, touch each egg. Remember to say only one number for each egg you touch.

Touch and count.

Touch and count.

Touch and count.

Now It's Your Turn

Count the little fish. Count aloud.

Start at the left and move to the right. Remember to say only one number for each fish you touch.

Touch and count.

Touch and count.

Touch and count.

Now It's Your Turn

Count the turtles. Count aloud.

Remember to say only one number for each turtle you touch.
Start at the left and move to the right.

Touch and count.

Touch and count.

Touch and count.

Practicing Together

Let's match numbers.

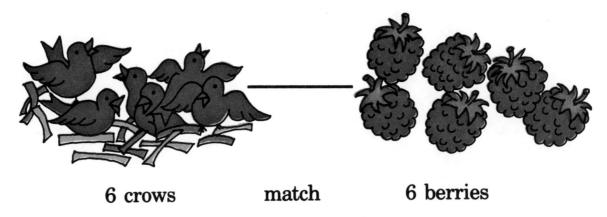

6 crows   match   6 berries

There is the same number of crows as berries. No matter how different they look, we can say they match in number. Because they match in number, we draw a line between them.

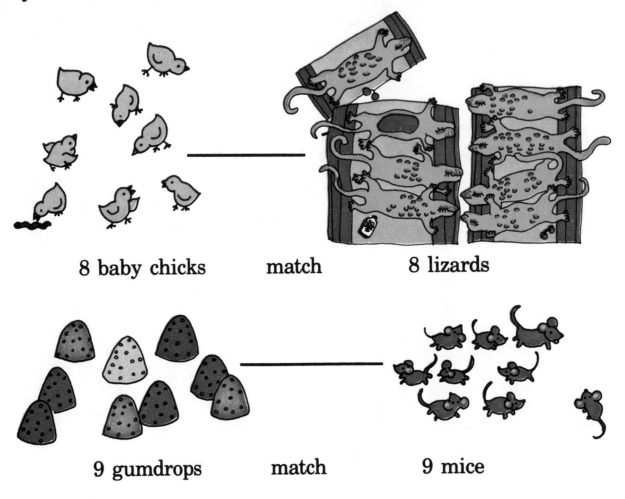

8 baby chicks   match   8 lizards

9 gumdrops   match   9 mice

Now It's Your Turn

Let's match numbers.

10 party hats

10 nuts

Draw lines between the groups that match in number.

7 frogs

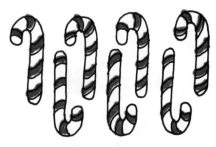

7 candy canes

9 pearls

9 ducks

8 apples

8 fish

Stop and Look

See how they match.

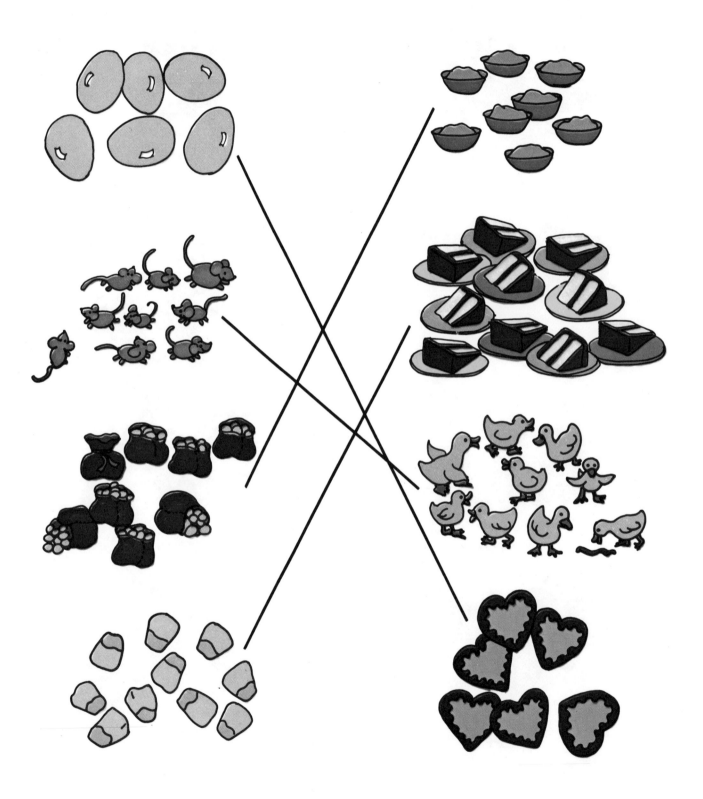

Now It's Your Turn

Draw lines between the groups that match in number.

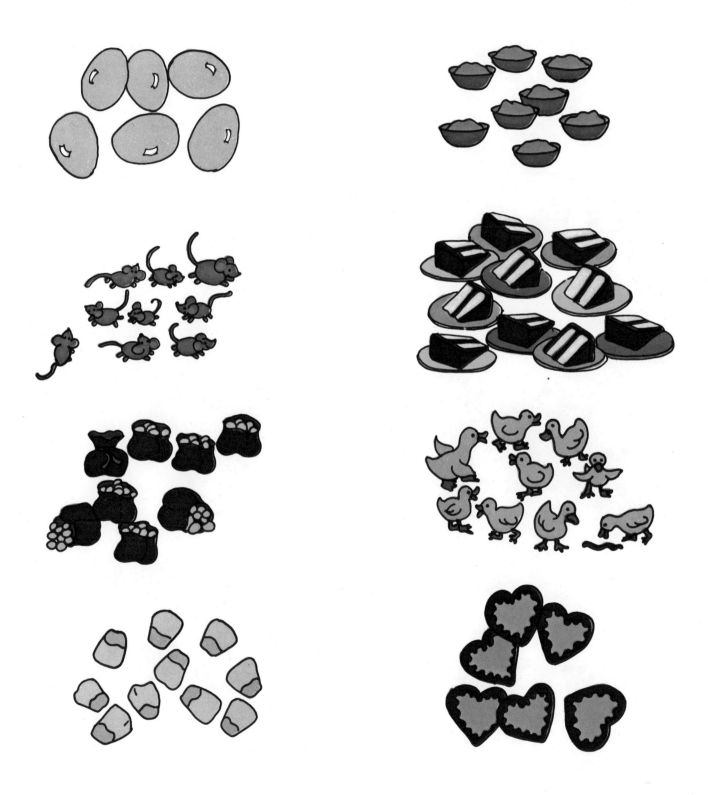

Now It's Your Turn

Practice writing numerals 6 and 7.

Trace these numerals. Remember to always start at the top.

6 ___ ___ ___ ___ ___

Write a numeral 6 on each line. Which 6 looks the best?

Trace these numerals. Remember to start at the top.

7 ___ ___ ___ ___ ___

Write a numeral 7 in each space. Which 7 looks best?

Stop and Look

Now It's Your Turn

Practice writing numerals 8 and 9.

Trace these numerals. Always start at the top.

8 ___ ___ ___ ___ ___ ___

Write a numeral 8 on each line. Which 8 looks the best?

Trace these numerals. Start at the top.

9 ___ ___ ___ ___ ___ ___

Write a numeral 9 in each space. Which 9 looks the best?

Stop and Look

Can you count the toes on both of your feet?

Can you shake your right leg 10 times?

Now It's Your Turn

Practice writing the numeral 10.

Trace these numerals. Remember to start at the top.

10 _____ _____ _____ _____

Write a numeral 10 on each line. Which 10 looks best?

6 7 8 9 10

Do you remember how to write these numerals?

_____ _____ _____ _____ _____

Now write the numerals 6 through 10.

Practicing Together

Count the boxes in each row.

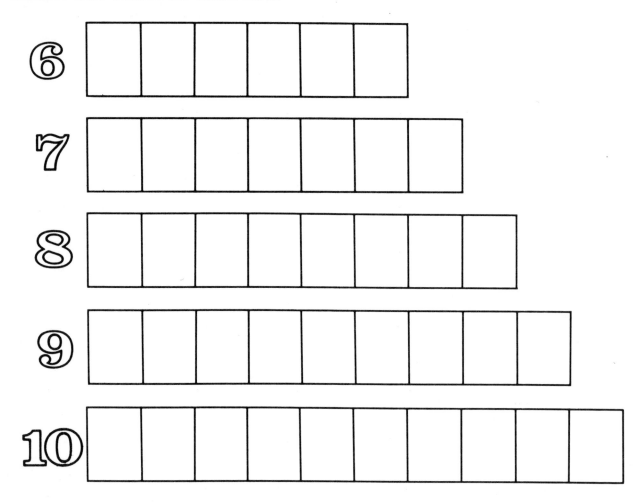

Can you see that each row has one more box than the row above it?

Which row has more boxes than any other row?

Did you pick the row with 10 boxes? This row has the most boxes.

Now It's Your Turn

Color the number of boxes in each row that matches the numeral.

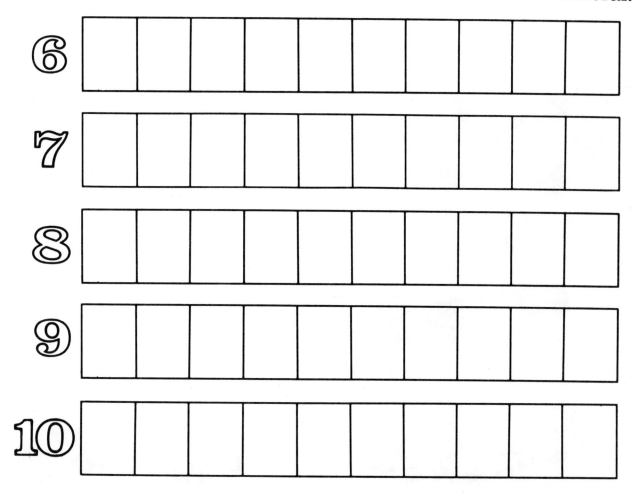

Each row should have one more colored box than the row above it.

Practicing Together

Touch and count.

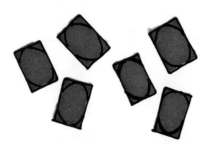

6 rubies

6 ducklings

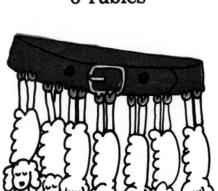

7 sheep

7 horns

8 apples

8 Indians

Now It's Your Turn

Touch, count and write the correct numeral in each box.

How many rubies? ☐

How many ducklings? ☐

How many sheep? ☐

How many horns? ☐

How many apples? ☐

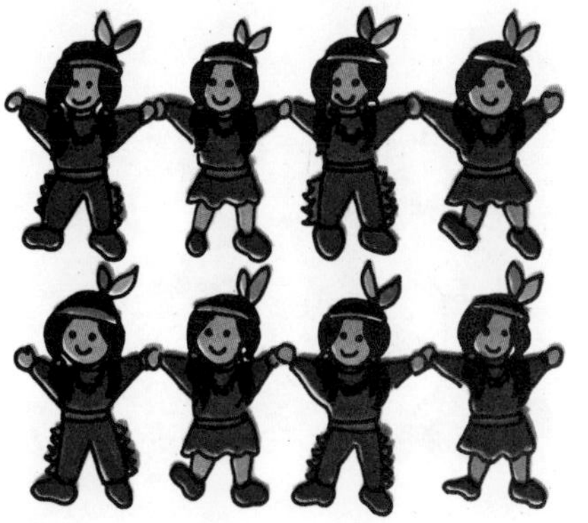

How many Indians? ☐

Practicing Together

Touch and count.

8 muffins

10 nuts

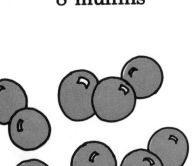

9 pearls

8 apples

10 party hats

9 ducks

Now It's Your Turn

Touch, count, and write the correct numeral in each box.

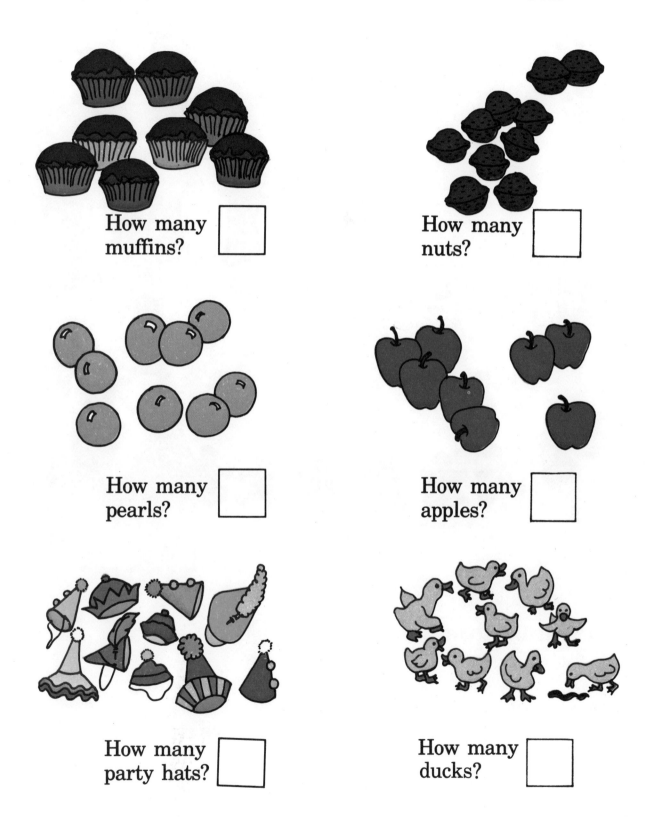

How many muffins?

How many nuts?

How many pearls?

How many apples?

How many party hats?

How many ducks?

Can you find these:

1 witch   2 children   3 trees   4 windows   5 birds

6 berries   7 candy canes   8 apples   9 gumdrops

10 gingerbread cookies

Now It's Your Turn

Touch, count, and draw lines to match the numbers.

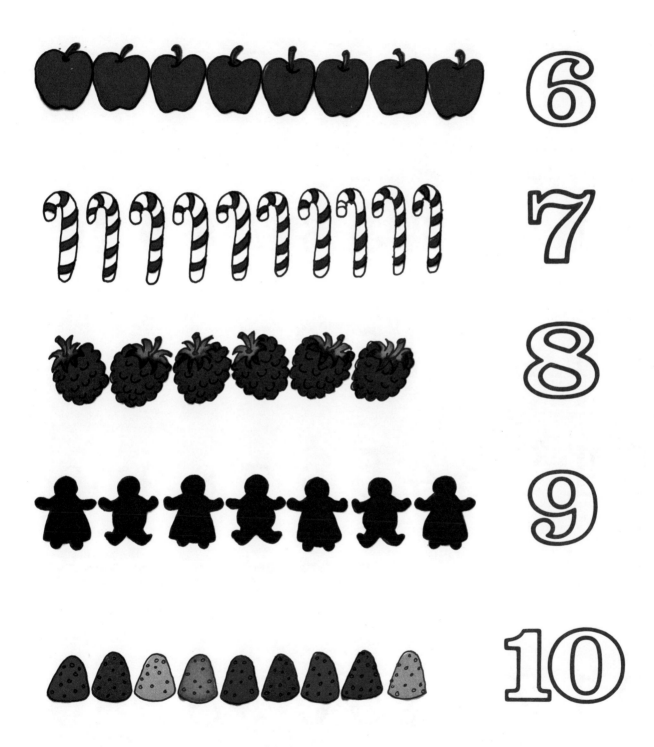

Practicing Together

Touch and count.

0 1 2 3 4 5 6 7 8 9 10

0 1 2 3 4 5 6 7 8 9 10

Count aloud the numbers that are written large. Whisper the numbers that are written small.

0 1 2 3 4 5 6 7 8 9 10

0 1 2 3 4 5 6 7 8 9 10

0 1 2 3 4 5 6 7 8 9 10

0 1 2 3 4 5 6 7 8 9 10

0 1 2 3 4 5 6 7 8 9 10

Now It's Your Turn

Write the missing numerals.

0 1 2 _____ 6 7 8 9 10

Did you write the numerals from 3 to 5?

0 1 2 _____ 8 9 10

Did you write the numerals from 3 to 7?

_____ 6 7 8 9 10

Did you write the numerals from 0 to 5?

0 1 2 3 4 _____

Did you write the numerals from 5 to 10?

_____

Did you write all the numerals from 0 to 10?

Can you count from 0 to 10? Yes, you can!

GAMES AND PUZZLES

Can you find the numeral hidden in each picture?

When Jack ran away from the ogre he dropped 10 gold coins. Can you find them?

Connect the dots and show Jack where he can keep his coins safe. Remember to start at the numeral 1.

Can you find the 6 ducklings hiding in the marsh?

Starting at the numeral 1, connect the dots to make your own duckling.

Can you find the 4 children playing in the park?

Connect the dots to find out what the children are looking for.
Remember to start at the numeral 1.

Can you find the numeral hidden in each picture?

Which nest has more eggs?

Did you pick the nest with brown eggs? There are 5 brown eggs but only 4 white eggs. 5 is more than 4.

Which of Jack's trees has the most fruit?

If you picked the tree with pears you are right. There are 6 pears but only 3 peaches and 5 apples. 6 is more than 3 or 5. The pear tree has the most fruit.

Help Hansel and Gretel find the shortest way home. Which path is the longest?

Flemingdon Park
Nursery School

144